THE MIND BEHIND THE FACE

Edited by

Andrew Head

First published in Great Britain in 1998 by
POETRY NOW
1-2 Wainman Road, Woodston,
Peterborough, PE2 7BU
Telephone (01733) 230746
Fax (01733) 230751

Copyright Contributors 1998

HB ISBN 0 75430 470 1
SB ISBN 0 75430 471 X

FOREWORD

Although we are a nation of poetry writers we are accused of not reading poetry and not buying poetry books: after many years of listening to the incessant gripes of poetry publishers, I can only assume that the books they publish, in general, are books that most people do not want to read.

Poetry should not be obscure, introverted, and as cryptic as a crossword puzzle: it is the poet's duty to reach out and embrace the world.

The world owes the poet nothing and we should not be expected to dig and delve into a rambling discourse searching for some inner meaning.

The reason we write poetry (and almost all of us do) is because we want to communicate: an ideal; an idea; or a specific feeling. Poetry is as essential in communication, as a letter; a radio; a telephone, and the main criteria for selecting the poems in this anthology is very simple: they communicate.

An admirable and agreeable selection of word portraits compiled into an engaging collection.

Talented poets describe people they admire, love or hate, the famous, the rich and the poor. They do so in a purposeful and successful fashion which will inspire and delight the reader.

The Mind Behind The Face is a notable book of poetry appealing to both the young and old generations.

CONTENTS

TRUE LOVE

True love
is like the warmth of summer's sun.
True love
is constant, does not wax or wane.
True love
shows compassion to those in pain.
True love
is never critical or harsh.
True love
consoles the broken heart.
True love
sometimes hides behind the mists of time only to reappear again.
True love
endures the complexities of life.
True love
is the greatest gift - you are my
True love

Patricia Clarke

MOTHER LOVE

I'd heard about a mother's love,
My friends all said it was good.
They spoke about cuddles and hugs and fun,
But I'd never known them and never would.

They talked of presents at Christmas time,
Decorations and presents and lots of sweets,
But I remained silent, for not for me
Was Christmas day a time for treats.

There was never a time when she said 'I love you.'
Never took my hand in her own,
Loving arms never held my small body,
No gesture of love was ever shown.

For me, there was only rejection,
And blame for all that went wrong.
So I crept into a shell of indifference,
And tried very hard to be strong.

I could never go to her with my fears,
Never share elation, or sorrow,
And it wasn't just how she felt that day,
She'd be the same as tomorrow.

She resented my marriage, my children, my life,
For two years she ignored my existence,
And I thought, even then, perhaps in time,
I'd rise above her resistance.

Now she is gone, and I shed no tears,
My heart doesn't grieve or pine.
There was no love for me in her life,
Now there's none for her in mine.

Margaret Fink

OF MARGARET MILLER

You're a lady of great understanding, your advice is invariably sound,
Unspoiled by wealth or position, your feet are set firm on the ground.
You are not an extravagant person, no one could accuse you of waste,
Your home, which you love, is quite simple, but arranged with
impeccable taste,
Independent are you and strong minded, outspoken and witty and
bright.
And you rarely complain of the devilish pain that's kept you awake half
the night.
You are loyal to your friends without question and gossip is something
you hate.
And if you have an appointment, you never like to be late.
You have that rare Sagittarian beauty, distinguished, yet gracious and
sweet.
And a smile that is so enchanting , you have the whole world at your
feet.
In all that you do you're a lady, with a strong love for your fellow man.
And you have a great sense of duty - to serve them whenever you can.
If I had four words to describe you, I'd say that you are 'all that is dear.'
And really the kind of person that everyone wants to be near.
You've suffered a lot in your lifetime, but God only chooses the best,
For he knows that we lesser mortals, would never stand up to the test.
But if love can help you a little and if friendship can lighten your load.
Take comfort in knowing you have them, for as long as you travel life's
road.
I loved you the first day I saw you, somehow you stood out from the
rest.
And I'm glad now I didn't ignore you, for my judgement was
right -
You're the best.

A V Painter

PORTRAIT

He squats on pavement
Cap on ground
'Come on *govnor*
Spare a pound'

His dog beside him
Sharing space
Looking at
Each passing face

Some look skywards
Some away
Embarrassed to be asked
To pay

Some are angry
Can't he work?
They could sit there
Duties shirk!

No more shaving
No more shower
No more wages
No more power

Sit and beg
And watch the feet
Trudging past them
On the street

No more fireside
No more wife
No more mortgage
No more strife?

Sonia Richards

MY HERO
(To Pete)

To me, you are the gentlest man
That ever walked the earth
To me you are the only man
Who has really proved his worth

You did the work I should have done
When I wasn't able to walk,
You put up with my ills and chills
And my incessant talk!

You take me wherever you go
Do my shopping, my garden and all
I think this is all wonderful
You shouldn't be at my beck and call

But I do really appreciate your care
I'm so thankful for all that you do
At the end of each day, I always say
'Thank God that I've got you!'

But one thing in life frightens me
That one day you'll want to go
I just pray this will never happen
Though I have no rights, I know.

Marjorie Wagg

THE MAIDEN AUNTS

Always wore lavender hand-knitteds,
Grey-haired and ageless,
They lived in a house on a hillside,
Carefully pruning and planting their sloping garden,
Fussed Mrs Tibbs with chicken and cream,
Went to chapel on Sunday.
Took me to tea in Rowntree's cafe,
Toasted tea-cake for a treat,
Watching the gulls over the bay.
Choreographed by time and habit,
Their life together a seamless harmony;
An extension of childhood playing house,
Continued into old age.
Nell died first,
Elsie, left alone, turned strange,
Hoarded candles and sugar,
And died in hospital
Calling for a lost secret lover.
Among the tidyings of the house,
A box of fancy gold scissors
And a card -
'Had a happy day out and bought ourselves these.'
Memories of a life - boxed and treasured.

Margaret Black

MICHAEL THE MARTYR

Michael the martyr
His life is a mess,
His spirit was shackled
By a thug in a dress!
Michael the martyr
Squandered his dreams,
But nobody knows him
He's not what he seems.
Michael the martyr
Stares down at the floor,
Can't bear being with her
Hangs out at the door.
Michael the martyr
Will he ever win?
Smiling in secret
At his private sin.
Michael the martyr
Will never confess,
Though he'd never admit it
He thrives on the stress!

Sally Malone

TIME TO LEAVE, MY CHILD

My arms are reaching out to you
They want to hold you tight
You glide across the sea of dreams
In which I drown each night
I've watched you gently blossom
With amazement and in awe
The world is spread before you
Step away now and explore

Kim Montia

PORTRAIT OF GRANDMOTHER

Sure, she was a princess, walking so gracious, as if on air.
she could sit on her so long and silky hair!
She was so rare; and never loud;
when we went to the fair, she stuck out from the crowd.

Her room filled with lavender scent, I shall never forget.
I had to share her with others, to my regret.
She told me, before she got married, she had a watch-chain
made out of her beautiful, light brown mane.

Being cuddled and squeezed to her chest,
the gentleness and her caring, I remember best.
Nan taught me how to knit, crochet, and cook;
never hurt, argued, always a smiling look.

She was so tall and slender,
no bother to her to bend over the fender.
Nan could laugh like nobody else,
It sounded like music, clear as a bell.

She was a storyteller too, thinking back;
she was great, really had the knack.
She, also, could sing like a bird in spring.
Nan had a refined mind, not many around of her kind.

Life without her was never the same.
Old age and a fractured hip were to blame.
All I know is, she was great.
Simply said: a *Supermate!*

Annenarie Poole

PORTRAITS

I'm hiding by the staircase,
As he's coming down the hall.
I don't think he can see me,
With my back against the wall.
I'm peering out to watch him pass,
To watch as he walks by.
And can just make out his figure,
From the corner of my eye.
He isn't much to look at,
Of that there's little doubt
With the stains upon his T-shirt,
And his label hanging out.
Although he has a little hair,
I can't say that it's much.
And what he has is greasy,
And not very nice to touch.
Many teeth are rotten,
Quite a few are gone.
You wonder how,
The ones that stay,
Can bear to carry on.
It's true to say he's overweight,
He's quite some pounds to lose.
But I don't think,
It would take him long,
If he'd just give up the booze.
Yet when all is said and done,
Despite him looking bad,
I'm afraid I can't reject him,
'Cause he'll always be my dad.

Louise Everitt

JACOB'S RONDEAU

I'm only two, but I can see
there's much to find beyond that tree.
I think it's time that I should run
and find the beach where there is sun.
My dad comes up and says to me:-
'My darling Jake it's time for tea,
another day we'll see the sea.'
'Oh no,' I scream, 'I want my fun,
I'm only two.'

I try to rush across the lea.
Oh dear! My fall has hurt my knee.
I yell and cry, 'I'd just begun
to reach that tree. What have I done?'
And then my mum reminded me
I'm only two.

Evelyn Golding

ONE MAN'S VOYAGE OF DISCOVERY

Twilight paints a tiny statue
ash brown, dove grey, dusky blue.
Hindsight reveals
brown curls, grey eyes, velvet dress.
Your smile entreats my caress,
guilt defeats my redress.
Moonlight strikes murky mists of time.
Whispered words promise sleep sublime;
aching bones recall ancient crime,
living winds vent their force,
drifting souls seek remorse.
Now I have somewhere to go
will my soul forgive and grow?
Are my eyes afraid to weep
now my heart declares dead sleep?
Daylight drapes illuminate
ash brown, dove grey, dusky blue.
Morning shapes reiterate
sad hair, wet lids, dusty hue.
Strangers prise knotted fingers,
strangled hope barely lingers,
release the statue - hope will decree
my ship is a tall ship sailing free.

Maureen Bold

THE DEVIL'S OWN

Hidden facade, you wore an unassuming shell
the devil's disciple straight from hell
spreading infection, leeching cancerous tumour
fooled into danger by your creeping humour
fuel for your sins, dark crimes buried deep
misguided innocents whose essence you keep
soul snatching lies, weaving your spell
victims tortured and beaten, hear the death knell
flesh of your flesh, the seed of your loins
killed by the malignancy of poisoned groins
poaching the lives of those you crave
rotting in silence, entombed in shallow grave
with eager killing hands you strangled life
black-hearted spouse, evil scheming wife
for passing years you preyed on the poor
cruelly escaping the chasing law
pursuing unhindered your shadowed calling
under the perpetual veil of darkness falling
finally evading justice, slipping the tether
suspended in death, tight hanging leather
accompanied by cold clinging shades
those you caressed with life-stealing blades
driven to suicide by fevered dreams
surrounded in solitude by splintered screams
drawn to your dark destiny ever faster
enveloped in flame, home with your master

Paul Birkitt

THE WORKER

Eyeing up a piece of wood,
he thumbs a trusty nail
and, though he hears the call to food,
he scarce imports the hail -
for his work is not yet done.

Tongue aside he concentrates,
considers each angle,
for carelessness alone he hates -
sloth makes his nerves jangle -
and the work which is not done.

With head wise beyond his years,
he hammers hard just so
and drives forth all his mother's fears
which did not want to go;
now David can feast, work done.

Phoenix Martin

LINDZY

There's a girl
I know not her name
Or from where she came,
She enters the room on no broom
But with such grace,
Always a smile on her face
So pleasant and warm,
A twinkle of light caught her eye
Illuminating her simple charm,
Calm and conserved,
Energies being preserved
Happy to stop and talk
company to keep,
That warm glow that comes
from deep inside,
A face you recognise
amongst the milling crowd,
Happy and proud,
A friend, smiling face
to recognise and converse with,
Brighten up my day
in such a kind way.

K M Clemo

A SIMPLE SMILE
(For my dear nephew, Samuel)

His fingers plunge into the darkness hunting for the unknown,
His golden hair shuffles as he plays.
His mysterious face holds the key to thousands
Of secrets that only he will ever realise.

His vivacious scent, up close,
Reminders of innocent youth mixed with perplexity.
The embers shining with immeasurable
Light as the most simple is complicated.

Seconds pass, a lifetime gained as
New intelligence blossoms into life.
So precious, so envied this babe child
As he glows like a new lit fire.

As instinctiveness calls for action
This creature boldly encompasses experience and trial,
So he emerges full grown from child cocoon
With ever growing patience and tenderness.

Child, more influential than any of his peers
Harnesses new life with vigorous vitality.
Youth now mature explodes into millions of pieces,
Shattering pain, producing a simple smile.

Michelle Corcoran

ROBOT MAN

A set of words fall together
And hit the bottom of my head
As hard as a brick
A useless attempt
At romance

The image is sickly
Traditional or complete
It is impossible
And thoughts choke
My impulse

Colleagues encourage and cajole
But my head is not responding
To their words or my feelings
The banging continues
I can't translate

John Carmody

FOR BETH, 18, WHO HANGED HERSELF

All the pain and anger
just beneath the skin
going on forever
deep so deep within

welling up inside me
trying to get out
I don't know how to deal with it
to let these feelings out.

I know that if they don't stop soon
it will be too late
it will rip apart inside of me
to let my feelings out.

I have cut myself to pieces
just to feel the pain
no feelings there, not there
I will have to try again.

I once thought you'd care for me
but things had gone too far
my spirit and my body
- just one big ugly scar.

Such feelings left inside me
I can't bear any more
nothing else can hurt me
I've seen it all before.

Does life go on forever
when you really want to stop?
What can I do to end it?
Maybe just one knot?

Sue Bomford

MICHAEL

Craggy face with eyes of hunted horror
That laugh on other days in other places.
Wild tension in his stillness tells a story,
Inside his head the world's a sea of faces.

Coarse brown hair, unshaven cheeks, black braces
Imply the tortured artist from the past
- This artist's tortured by his fears, remembering
Those childhood days when bitter dice were cast.

Chewed-down nails round coffee cup are curling,
Skin's pale as ice and slack lips gently dance.
Confused and acid words come spewing outwards,
Constricted by that fierce intelligence.

Every picture tells a horror story
Yet still the backbone's straight, the eyes are bright.
Some days he wants to drown in this near-madness
Yet every day he's made it through the night.

Liz Proctor

LETTER TO FANNY

When I go round the world
On the great, grand tour
I shall only flirt with gentlemen
That are elegant and pure.

Mother says the things downstairs
Are all right in their way
But one mustn't get too close
As they take your breath away.

Our gardener died last week,
I couldn't shed any tears
He was a crippled old crone
Who'd been with us for years.

Sunday was really exciting
Father whipped a drunken man
The horses had to slow down
It rather spoiled our plan.

We were galloping through the
Street, not wanting to be late
The sermon was awfully good
'Strong drink is the devil's state.'

I've sent the maid collecting
You should have seen the look,
I shall spend the afternoon
Pressing nature in a book.

Mother's head of another committee
Concerned with urchins in need.
Bring me some miniatures from Venice
Enjoy the tour and Godspeed.

Maureen Macnaughtan

JACKIE

J oyous is the lady who gives not up
A nd fares beyond all hope in every drama;
C ourageously taking Honours, she gave her all
K eeping lectures in hand whilst being mum.
I in awe, stand. So much she would juggle.
E ternal her friendship I hold so dear.

Richard Cole

A PORTRAIT OF MY FATHER

Such a gentle man, whose kind and generous spirit outshone the
                                                sunniest days.
A wit whose humour in the extreme, spoke volumes of his sense
                                                of the ridiculous;
Laughter reigning throughout the house, when hobbies were set
                                                aside for a while.
His talents, boundless, be they of a house-maintenance,
Or green-fingered nature, he always knew, just how to do, and just
                                                what to do,
Each task in a particular and the correct way,
Perfection was the end result, no matter how long the task lasted.
As a child the house was LOCO orientated,
His model steam engines individually built to scale,
I would watch him copy every detail, from the blueprint pinned to
                                                his drawing board,
Brass carefully cut and turned on his lathe, then polished lovingly.
Being young I did not understand the concentration and degree of
                                                difficulty concerned,
My incessant chatter, must have driven him mad,
But not once did he shout, always the soft voice, answering my naive
                                                questions.
Music was ever present, be it Sinatra, Jelly Roll Morton or Bix
                                                Beiderbeck,
The famous clarinet would appear and the dulcet tones would echo
                                                through each room,
I recall those familiar sounds, even now I can hear them clearly in
                                                my head.
He was a master, a genius, nothing was too much, he would mull over
                                                a problem,
No matter how complex and decipher the best form of attack, the result
                                                was always right.
The admiration and respect I still have for him, will never leave me.
There was a special bond, words were not our forte, but there was
                                                understanding,

I remember him often, I miss him still dreadfully,
Even after these five long years;
I can still see him wearing his navy blazer, walking towards me,
                              as I park my car,
On a sunny afternoon, when we would take tea in the garden,
                              under the apple tree.

A L Manning

MY FATHER; MY FATHER

My Father; my Father
May my life be an example to many;
to tell of Your awesome love
and may many come to know;
Your loving kindness and Your grace
upon those You call Your own

My Father; my Father
how great You are, my Father
with loving kindness You comfort me
with tenderness You cover me
over and over;
with the great strength You possess

My Father; my Father
You showed me the paths You take
and the roads You have made;
specially for me
You have worked out so great a salvation
for my soul to save
I can come boldly to Your throne of grace
to bow down and worship Your name

My Father . . .my Father
may I never leave Your loving presence
all the days of my life
I will teach my children
to walk at all times in Your paths . . . my Father
so they can walk in the wondrous ways
You have set for their little feet
My Father . . . my Father.

Patricia Aboagye

THE STRANGER

There once was a beautiful stranger
who walked through the village alone!
She moved with the grace of a panther,
Her eyes shone like emeralds and gold.
Her skin was like finest bone china,
Her hair, it was blacker than coal
Her feet were so small and so dainty -
On her finger a band made of gold!
For this was no ordinary stranger
Who walked through the village alone,
As heads turned, and all eyes were upon her,
Only she knew this really was home!
For a long time ago she had left them,
For a better life far, far away
Now more happy, contented and peaceful -
She knew that she never could stay.
So she walks through the streets like a stranger
So glad she is finally free,
And the village folk still talk in whispers
Of the beautiful stranger they see.

Charmaine S Dawson

FOR GARETH

How evil is the arrogance that feeds your swollen pride,
more evil still your well of hate, in which a child has died.
obsession clothed in bitterness your battles never lost,
you wallow in your triumph watching those that count the cost.

What say you now as darkness comes what say you now to need?
The tears of God were not enough to satiate your greed.
Tortured souls fall in your wake to feed your giddy head,
till sadness visits sorrow, where the angels fear to tread.

What say you now for all the lies that flow so easily?
What say you to your triumphs cloaked in cunning and deceit?
The hidden veil of darkness holding faces that you preen,
still finds you strutting outside, inside; no one ever sees.

What say you now for Gareth as you still revile his dad,
the one he always needed, but was too afraid to have?
How evil is the arrogance that feeds your swollen pride,
more evil still your well of hate, in which a child has died.

Steve Percy

MY FRIEND

I remember well the days of long gone by
when I was yet still young
with spirits strong and high;
Then I had a friend
who walked life's path with me.
She always saw the rights and wrongs
that I could never see.

Though our paths divided still she lingers on
following in the shadow
of the good times that have gone;
She's there to lend a listening ear
when others turn away,
And offer a helping hand
to lighten a burdened day.

Many a tear she's shed to mingle with mine own
when saddened and depressed
and very much alone;
Many a laugh she's shared
when heavy skies have cleared,
And the fettered heart is freed
from the pain so sorely seared.

Now that life is good my friend she'll always be
Loyal and unerring
caring faithfully;
Dearly, then I love her
for such loyalty
And thank God for lending
such a friend to me.

A V Garner

INTERMISSION

Where is the girl
Who played in morning's sun,
With cherub's face
And angel's wing,
Who baked me sweetened mud pies
In her mother's best rose dishes,
On sparrow's legs
With fledgling smiles
Along with sticks of fun,
And made me pretend to eat them
One by one;
Who counted my golden whiskers
As if they were the days to come,
To fly
The nesting reeds of sun;
Yes, where is the girl
Who played in beams just spun,
With cherub's face
And angel's wing?
Why she has just grown up to ever stay
And gone,
Gone,
Gone,
Oh! So far away.

Norman Royal

PORTRAIT

You left
It was sudden,
without warning
Why?
Was she more beautiful more caring than I?

My life now empty, drained of emotion
Remembers days filled with fun and commotion
of children's laughter, smiles and tears
Their leaving home
My worries, your fears

Now you are gone
Just an empty space
But mirrored before me
I see always your face

A face whose eyes look without shame
A face whose eyes reveal suffering and pain
A face with features strong and rugged
A furrowed brow, sometimes troubled

Your words outspoken,
some harsh, some kind
A man determined,
never changing your mind
You were my rock
Dependable, unchanging
Always providing a firm foundation

But I faltered, I stumbled my way along
Now your chair is empty, your clothes all gone
The tears I have cried, the loss, the pain
Will I ever find my true love again?

Jennifer Polledri

SWEETEST LOVE

Your smile is my sunshine,
Your lips are my wine.
Your voice is my songbird,
Your eyes are my guide,
Your words are my lifeline,
Your love is my life.

Anna King

UNTITLED

Words are sometimes hard to find
To express the feelings I have inside
A love so pure and so true
Is the love I have for you
My loving Lord how can I explain
That you ease all my stress and strain
You lift me up and hold me high
You give me wings so I can fly
You do so much what can I do
But give my heartfelt thanks to you.

Lynda Hippsley

RELATIVELY SPEAKING

Mother-in-law is coming to tea,
I wonder which hat
she'll be wearing today,
there's a store-cupboard full
for each change of her mind,
- of instant disguises,
hats all shapes and sizes -
and two she reserves
- just for me.

> If she's flaunting the straw one,
> shiny and black,
> prickly and prim,
> with a bow at the back,
> bristling with candour
> from crown to sharp brim,
> then I'll know
> that she's gunning for me.

But, if she's bedecked
in a froth of pink tulle,
coquettishly perched
in a candyfloss twirl,
then I'll know that the dragon
has sanctioned the girl
- in her heart -
to be chummy with me.

> So I'm cleaning in corners and polishing chairs,
> to counter the custom of clinical stares:
>
> and shopping, and baking, and waiting to see,
> which facet of fashion is coming to tea.

June White

ELLEN

The epitome of kindness, love was all around
The family adored her, we were on common ground
My mother's elder sister, Constance Ellen was her name
A refuge for a troubled soul, she wouldn't claim the fame

Her hair was curly, dark and short, bright eyes and fetching specs
Smart blouses, pearls and earrings, a credit to her sex.
Womanly, broadminded, wise, consistent, liked some fun
She made a fuss of everyone, loved her marzipan

Small in stature, huge in heart, a Christian by her acts
Understanding, positive, with or without the facts
So very unassuming, delightful in her way
Admired and respected, more than words can say

A lady from our working class, untarnished by a war
Had an aura with her, even with the shortest straw
Made family life so easy, cared so much for others
In fact, in many ways, she was the queen of busy mothers

No bad words, a compromise, there is a reason why
A gentle heart, a peacemaker who wouldn't hurt a fly
Enjoyed life in the countryside, loved walking in the lanes
Was happy with the basic life, no fast cars or planes

Forgot to say that she was ill, the news was very bad
We said goodbye, she passed away, we were very, very, sad
Her memory will never die, the feeling is so strong
Her name hangs softly on the breeze, like a never-ending song.

B M Hurll

TEA BARMY

When it's cold and wintry
Or hot and steamy
I'll have a cup of tea.
Strong or weak it doesn't matter to me
Just so long as it's very sweet.
You know it's an invaluable treat
Meet the trouble and strife,
Diane, the wife.
Not the most intelligent so to speak
But her tea is quite unique,
Without it I would freak.
'Will you brew me a cuppa?' I'd ask.
'On my way, without delay.' she'd say.
She would do this eleven times a day
At home I thought she would stay,
But she ruined my life.
By running off, with someone else's wife!
Now I drink coffee
Because of my late, lonely nights.
Waking up tired as a mite,
But I still love her despite
Although it was the cups of tea I liked.

Ali Sebastian

BUSTER

A dog that chewed up all our socks,
Unwrapped and ate our Christmas chocs;
Was pushed in a pram in dollies' frocks
Buster - our family dog.

Who flew through the air and grabbed your toast
And once made off with the Sunday roast;
Who was cock of the street - or so we would boast.
Buster - our family dog.

Who chased the postman with much vigour
And lady dogs of any figure.
Who could make a hole bigger than a mechanical digger.
Buster - our family dog.

How I wish he was still there
To trip me up and make me swear
And cover my nice clean cushions with hair.
Buster - our family dog.

But now he's gone and there's only me.
I buried him under the old fruit tree.
I eat the pears and think of he.
Buster - our family dog.

Carol Fenlon

TERRY MY BROTHER . . . A PORTRAIT

My world fell apart on the day you died,
I filled my own ocean, with the tears I cried.

Your laughter-filled eyes, your ever smiling lips,
Your handsome bronzed face, never again to be kissed.

Your sparkling shining smile, lighting up a room,
Where if you did not enter it . . . would exist doom and gloom.

Your treatment of all humankind, with tenderness and care,
Treating all as equals . . . you had so much love to share.

Forever young at heart, forever playing the fool,
Adored by all your pupils, when you taught them at school.

'Live life to the full' was your motto, 'don't just exist,'
This you did with zeal, you truly got your wish.

A light has gone out, *never* to be replaced by another,
For no-one else can take the place of *my dear brother*.

Tracy Bell

SINGING FOR LUIS PALAU (HOUNSLOW HEATH)

Leaving the tent and the moonlit heath,
To catch the 10.05 bus by the pub,
After an evening with Luis Palau;
I turn to view the lit-up tent,
And the deep dark blue sky.
- To hear the singing of *Our God Reigns;*
I have never heard, and seen, a sight so marvellous.

G A Burgess

NO MORE!

Still now, your hands,
In memories sensations
I feel tightening
around my throat,
On your burning hatred,
In fear,
I glimpsed darkness
As I choked,
Pressure welling
deep within my head,
Could not breathe,
Blackness, signalling,
My own impending death,
So often the scenario,
As you beat me,
Images of my life,
my mind's eye could see.
Your testament of love,
Such agonising torture,
Covered in bruises,
black and ugly,
I was not taught, that this,
Was how love should be,
You crying,
Pleading, the promises,
Giving anything
Hoping I would not leave,
I with swollen eyes,
Bags in hand,
Crying children
Pulling desperately on my sleeve,
Through your suffocations,
I yearned to be free,

Never wanting to be the punch-bag,
Who would be cowed,
So full of future regrets,
Later when I had grown old,
Would I have grown old?

Elaine Hawkins

THE LITTLE MOUSE

Her face is etched with an
intricate pattern of lines -
some quite deep furrows
where her chin declines.
Others, a network
of slight criss-cross
running into each other
until you are at a loss
of where each one started
and ended. Upon her brow
two frown-lines, so deep -
a worried look, somehow.
Her eyes, small and bright,
flick briefly, nervously, around.
Her voice, when heard, so quiet,
afraid to make a sound.
Her nose, so long and thin,
quivers like a dog on scent.
The glasses, straddled across,
are battered, old and bent.
Perched on the edge of her chair
she seems ready to take off -
and every so often
gives a nervous little cough.
We wonder why she ever comes -
perhaps she's old, alone?
Perhaps she hasn't any friends
with whom to have a moan?

J Hockley

MINNA

Amidst a sea of posies and mouse-eared grasses
in a cottage garden I see a sweet forget-me-not face
framed by a bonnet of calico - round about four, her age is
smocked in cornflower-blue with smocking interlaced.

She seems quite at home among a profusion of nature
garlanded by flowers of each and every hue
mossy-red roses with honeysuckle climbing festooning
scarlet pimpernel - muscari and periwinkle blue.

There are lupins - lilies and wide-eye ox daisies
jolly stocks and hollyhocks - iris of pale blue
white dianthus under sweet williams gazes
foxgloves and kitten-eyed pansies peek-a-boo.

Yet the fairest flower among them all
is the darling bud called Minna
with a tiny basket in her hand - a little petal
heading for the seed heads - happy gardening sweet beginner.

Lucy Green

ON MY GRANDMOTHER

She chained herself to the railings
in Hyde Park for Votes for Women,
and was put in prison and fed
bread and water.

She wrote a book about her life
in India as wife of a magistrate.

She talked, told stories of snakes,
and held noisy cocktail parties.
To the age of ninety-four
she was fit and sociable.

Always welcoming, but with a critical
eye for truth and youth, she
was one of a breed which knew
no bounds.

Keith Murdoch

THE BOXER

Money
flash cash, not enough
fuelling ego
strutting your stuff
proud gladiator
adulation and fame
former champ
there lies the blame
baying crowd
fading glory
fight fans fury
false end to the story
hard pounding gloves
age battered flesh
raw bruising power
eye closing fresh
bloodied skin
primed for a fall
standing firm
you've given your all
hopes duly raised
back in the groove
hurting pain
nothing to prove
passion still burning
let sleeping dogs lie
integrity restored
retire on a high
family to thank
saving Eubank

Chris Bailey

CAREERS' INTERVIEW

When it was time for my interview
I had no idea how important the man was.
He asked me to sit down
And said he had once met my father.
Then he got rather business-like,
Sort of all at once.
He said he had studied my case
And that if I played ball with him
There could be something in it for me.
I wasn't too quick
To see what he was driving at
But it sounded fishy.
I mean he didn't look shifty
But you could tell something was up.
Then he began to give me very precise information.
He said he would sketch the job possibilities for me
So next he began to talk
And he certainly could talk.
It was as if he'd said it lots of times before
And he kind of looked through me,
All the time looked through me
As I listened
To his rather slick and competent performance.

Alasdair Aston

THE OBESE

He steadily increased in weight;
It was his nature to be great,
But can his big heart tolerate?
Will not his belly ulcerate?

His friends pretended to be wise:
Each one was eager to advise;
His figure could bear no disguise,
Nor he the portents of demise.

'Check your cholesterol level,
Fats and uric acid gravel,
Thin your sugar with a shovel,
Must death join you on your travel?'

'Attend a slimming club and train:
We bet you will be thin again;
Begin to lose a stone or twain:
Your fat will slither down the drain.'

Was that all their conversation,
Just to increase his frustration?
Bigger men are in the nation
Who feel greater consternation.

His friends all died in turn, each one,
But he outlived their jokes and fun
And when his work on earth was done,
He said his farewell to the sun.

It was when he, an old man, died,
One digger to another cried,
'Make sure the grave is deep and wide:
This man is big from side to side.'

S K Haddad

ENIGMA

I'll guide you on a journey,
where none have gone before,
there will be many obstacles
before we reach the core.

This wall you face is solid,
or so it would appear,
to overcome this barrier
chase away the fear.

The path ahead is tangled,
stay close and do not stray,
I fear it would be easy
for you to lose your way.

This maze, I know, seems endless,
though the clues are there to see,
the gates are all around us
and compassion is the key.

That building is a fortress,
defence from any harm,
to enter through the portals
you must first disarm.

Through corridors and hallways,
through many coloured doors,
passed walls depicting life scenes
and ever changing floors.

Our journey's almost over,
we approach the centre here,
that light ahead is what we seek
the source will soon be clear.

You look upon a secret now,
and none have found the key,
for there encased in crystal
is the essence that is me.

Mandy Rossiter

MARIE AND ME

We played in the park Marie and me
and I told her the tale of the 'fairy tree'.
Here they come to dance and sing,
and over there is the fairy ring.

Brown eyes looked at me with such delight
as I told her the tales from morn to night.
We'd lie on the grass and gaze at the tree,
and dream of the places we'd like to see.

Shall we ride on a moonbeam or go on a star,
to the magic land where the fairies are?
So we'd dream where none could see.
just the two of us Marie and me.

The years slipped by and we went our ways
with homes of our own and families to raise.
The fairy tree so far away
Was just a dream of yesterday.

Then we talked it over Marie and me
and said it's time for us to see
some of the places so far away.
So we started to seek them feeling so gay.

We don't ride on a moonbeam or go on a star,
there's no fairies to greet us, wherever we are.
We've seen lots of places and met lots of folk
and know, to our families we are just a joke.

What they don't know and cannot see,
the *magic's* still there for *Marie and me.*

May Cleary

SUNDAY AFTERNOON

In the garden
under the heather, the cat sleeps,
We sit in the sunlight
reading, relaxing,
Next door, Vivaldi hurries along,
Over the fence, Oscar
yaps, furiously,
Jenny, next door
rages at small son.
The thud of a ghetto blaster
from God knows where
underlies all other sounds.
Smell of paraffin, burning fat,
from Linda's barbecue
overcomes the fragrance of flowers.
The cry of the lawnmower is heard in the land!
We retreat behind closed windows and doors,
and remember long gone summer days,
when people were considerate,
and Sunday afternoon peaceful.

Robert E Fairclough

THE VIRGIN YEARS OF YOUTH

The virgin years of youth unfolds
the innocent of mind,
and opens up the complexity,
of life to all mankind.

Girlfriends, boyfriends,
Country walks.
Exploring each other
with powerful talk.

A time for travel,
for we are young and free.
We have come of age and know it all,
so you old ones listen out for me.

If you should see me in the street,
just kindly step aside.
Or we may shout abuse at you
or poke you in the side.

Smashing cars and fences,
taking drugs and drink.
These virgin years of youth,
their minds are on the blink.

John Hickman

UNTITLED

Each day's the same
I'm getting bored
feels like I'm being strangled with a telephone cord
I look out the window
I look at the view
The grass is green and the sky is still blue
I'll get on the bus
I'll look for employment
But I know the outcome, they'll be no enjoyment
Same old dinner
Same old food
Same old telly makes me feel blue
Remembering my memories
Remembering my friends
All good things must come to an end
Each day's the same.

Frank Perry

REMEMBER ME

Remember me when I'm gone,
For good reasons and not wrong,
Will you think of me with kind heart?
Even though we're far apart.

Many times in my life I know,
To tell you of the love I couldn't show,
It hasn't been easy in my life,
To struggle on with all the strife.

I know I have been hard to please,
But, still you cannot perceive,
That I will remain in your memory,
For I know that you may just miss me.

It hasn't been easy for either of us,
All I need to do, is go with no fuss,
Just remember me when I'm gone,
I didn't just live, I did belong!

Denise Bracey

My Child

Rushing round in frantic frenzy,
> that's me from morn till night.
Your cheeky face and bright blue eyes
> sparkle mischievous delight.
Trying Mummy's patience
> is a game much played by you,
And teasing baby brother
> is your special talent too.
Tantrums are a must
> when you can't get your own way;
Mum's ready for bed before you are
> at the end of every day.
I'm sure I've aged a decade
> since the stork brought you along,
But even so I can't stay mad at you
> for very long.
'Cos you're really very special
> with your funny little ways.
Your expressions so unique
> warm so many of my days.
As I watch you whilst you're sleeping;
> full of love, I am beguiled,
For I know how blessed I am
> to have God's precious gift,
> > a child.

Alison Hulme

My Mother Tree

I've heard of pruning
but this is ridiculous!
Where were you master gardener
when callous-handed vandals
or unskilled under-gardeners
mutilated this my mother tree
hacking off here a bough of memory
there a branch of thought
reducing at a most ungentle stroke
to its lopsided shadow
this seasoned, shapely oak
bridge between earth and sky
generous shade and shelter
for countless creatures?

Perhaps
there is no master gardener
or he's capricious
having his good days and his bad
or just incompetent
unable to control what's gong on?

Or else
mysteriously
you are
in charge
effecting
the piecemeal
transplanting
of our whole blighted woodland
to your unpolluted forever forest
where every tree will be twig perfect.

Jean Watson

AGELESS

He hung with desperation to the leather strap.
His eyes were gazing sightlessly
Into the past. His loose-limbed movements
Swaying with the jolts;
Waiting for his stop;
Echoing his faults.

I watched his head hang past his years,
And wondered what had hurt him so inside.
His pride was there no more, but lying dusty
On the bus floor with his eyes.

His neck was red with recent shaving,
Rough and angry, there across his throat
He bore the mark of bitterness;
The pale pink line that spoke in silence -
Eloquent with stitch-mark punctuation -
Of a knowledge quite beyond his earth-bound time.

His face was young; his ancient mind
Knew only when to leave - he rang the bell.
The bus heaved to a stop with open doors
To welcome his departure;
He descended in one motion
And his eyes had never lifted from the floor.

T Hulligan

ELEONORA

She flits from art to human rights,
then Genesis, polluted streets,
Tchaikovsky's fifth, the price of bread
and Iliescu's nonsenses;
forgets to make the tea.

That marked December stained with blood,
she marched beside Romania's youth,
savoured eggshell freedom till
unnested by the cuckoo's wiles;
the boiling water spent.

Selecting blue and white bone china,
she pours out secrets of survival,
shares her heart, condemns barbaric years
which soured her nation's spirit;
serves fresh lemon tea.

Joanna Watson

SILENT WORLD

I wish I knew your thoughts
Sweet brother of mine
Locked in your own world -
Space and time.

You have never spoken,
But with eyes so blue
Gazed fixed upon me
I know that you
Remember who I am
Sweet brother of mine.

Bright colours, soft music
Make you smile,
Somewhere in your being
Is the key
To unlock this autistic world
And let you truly see -
Me
Sweet brother of mine.

Mary Lewis

AILEEN

I heard a young bride sing
So many years ago,
She sang a song called 'Young at Heart',
That made my tears flow.

She sang with such pathos
My child-heart it touched so,
She gave that song such meaning,
Those eyes seemed all aglow!

Those eyes so full could see not,
Diabetes claimed her sight,
Her older groom was blind from birth,
It seemed a sorry plight!

Her voice was clear and bell-like,
Each word from her soul came,
We all shared in her happiness
Of new-found joy - it's plain.

Yet there, she sang for him
Of happiness supreme,
They'd bought a house for two,
What courage! What a dream!

She died a few months later,
Fate can be so unkind,
Where're I hear 'Young at Heart',
I hear her in my mind.

She showed me how to live,
So never to grow old,
Happiness through little things
Is precious - more than gold!

Lola Perks-Hartnell

OLD AGE

The poor old dear
Is in a bad way,
Her eyes are dim,
She cannot hear.

Her legs are wobbly
At the knees,
Her hands are shaking
Like a leaf.

Her skin is wrinkled
Like an old dried prune,
She has no teeth
To chew her food.

She croaks like a frog
With a smile on her face,
Then laughs out loud
And her body sways.

Her bones are all rusty,
Her engine's wearing out,
She won't live much longer,
Of that I've no doubt.

So visit her this week,
Give her a treat,
Take chocolate and flowers,
And stay a few hours.

Hetty Foster

WORD PORTRAIT - THE DIY MAN

He's great at climbing ladders,
He can balance brush and can,
Every home should have one!
An agile DIY man!

He can decorate a ceiling,
And then re-hang a door,
Put up some useful shelving,
Or carpet the lounge floor.

He can make some fancy shutters,
Or unblock a smelly drain,
And then clean out the gutters,
Get ready for some rain.

He can re-tile the bathroom,
Or plumb in a shower,
Your choice now is quick splash
Or soak for an hour!

If your need is wiring
He'll prove he's a spark,
Who cares if he puts
Half the town in the dark!

He can sand down the floorboards
Or rebuild a wall,
In fact he will tackle
All jobs - big or small!

Now my pet DIY man
Is known both near and far,
But please do not let him
Near my precious car!

Ann Clowes

IN GRANNY'S DAY

In Granny's day one did not swear
My dear, you would not even dare.
When only doing this or that
Of course one always wore a hat.
And petticoats were pristine white,
One's tea gown gossamer and light.
Madeira cake was served for tea,
The children in the nursery.
The maids would bob in quaint respect,
No less than Granny would expect.
And we pretended not to look
When Grandpapa winked at the cook.

How swift the years to claim our youth
And age embroiders over truth,
The care assistant comes at two
To serve my lunch, it's always stew.
I've only memories to sustain
The slowing of my heart and brain
And folks may tire to hear me say
Just how it was in Granny's day.

Such a privilege for me
Born in an age of chivalry,
When gentlemen would come to call
To take a lady to a ball.
Or else to luncheon at the Ritz
With Algernon, Hubert and Fitz.
I know as visitors take their leave
They think it's only make-believe.
I don't know what they all would say
If they had lived in Granny's day.

Margaret Marklew

THE RECLUSE

Her eyes are small and almost shut,
Furrows line her forehead, but
These lines are not from worry drawn -
By foul bad temper they were born
No kindly words will pass her lips,
No friendly 'hello' or witty quips.

The mouth that presses lips together
In firm straight line, has seldom, if ever
Broken into a sunny smile
Or even relaxed for just a while.
Any words she has to say
Are spoken in a spiteful way.

Weather-worn skin and drawn back hair,
Wealth she has - but not to share.
Living alone is her own choice,
Scolding anyone who makes a noise.
Children shun her, animals scurry,
Making their getaway in a hurry.

When she walks beyond her gate
All that she projects is hate.
Oh how sad it seems to me
To be as crotchety as she.

Gina Whittle

PASSING STRANGERS

I only left the house for an hour
Some ordinary Friday evening,
Drifting in the gentle remnants of spring,
And then he came, riding into my solitude
Like a rude awakening astride steel and chrome,
Like an adventure of my life didn't need.

I only went dancing because I couldn't sleep
For the music was a symphony in my soul
And the city lights were poised
Like an orchestra above the river;
And he came pirouetting like an
Untouchable angel among the broken people.

I only came outside to catch the sun
Because I was frozen and the garden
Looked like a sanctuary one flaming June,
And in the street brown-skinned children played
But I was a forgotten orphan of winter.

Morning light, just a few hours away;
I only came outside to feel the stillness,
Standing in the confines of this slumbering,
Sightless and unknowing neighbourhood,
I knew his car, the question of his glance,
Like a loose connection, like an almost . . .

Paula Morris

THE DREAMS OF MISS MCKENZIE

Miss Dora McKenzie rose from bed
And scratched with skinny hand a head
No longer boasting tresses gold.
She shivered though it wasn't cold.
Her mirror showed she looked a sight
Unlike her favourite dream last night
When in her looks and dress and ways
She became as in her girlhood days.
A lovely dream where youthful feet
Had run through summer meadows sweet.
Where laughing couples climbed the stiles
And babbling brooks ran on for miles.
Where relatives long gone before
Appeared as through a magic door
And grouped themselves into a scene
That very long ago had been.
Miss Dora McKenzie heaved a sigh
And said to herself, 'I wish that I
Could bring about such dreams at will
And make the best in time stand still.'
Then Miss McKenzie settled down
Wrapped in her threadbare dressing gown
To sort the matters of the day.
She looked at all the bills to pay.
Her best loved bits would have to go.
At least, she thought, it's good to know
However dreary my life seems
No one can take away my dreams.

June Marshall

The Unsung Heroes

Every morning he is there, season ticket in his hand.
Wearing a dark business suit; collects his paper from the stand.

Every morning of the week. Rain or shine, year after year.
Waiting for the city train; his once smooth face lined with care.

Here comes the seven twenty-nine, and soon he's on his weary way
To dull routine and petty tasks; another tedious working day.

His paper unread on his knee, he shuts his eyes and quietly dreams
Of past ambitions quenched by life. Long-forgotten hopes and schemes.

He sees a rugged mountain high. Snow-capped, untouched by man
or time
Unchallenged peak, lost in cloud; the one he'd always hoped to climb.

He smells the salt tang of the sea, feels the roll and pitch and swell.
Pits his strength against the ocean; touches Heaven, glimpses Hell.

He sees a man whose life is full; master of his destiny.
Who lives each moment as his last; his mind alert, his spirit free.

The train grinds to a halt and then our friend wakes from his reverie.
Gone are the hopes of yesterday; back to harsh reality.

Pay the mortgage; meet the bills. Thrust all secret dreams aside.
Working at a job that bores, to meet the basic needs of life.

There are many men like this around. Plodding on from day to day.
What glorious feats might have been theirs had opportunity smiled
their way.

Who are the heroes of the world; the ones who climb and sail and roam,
And having done just what they wished with loud acclaim are
welcomed home?

Or all the countless millions who, unrecognised, unsung, unknown,
Must daily face monotony and with courage carry on . . .?

Valerie Wynn

NEW MUM BLUES

I've no identity left, I'm a mother, a wife
The person inside me is struggling to find life
A life outside of these four lonely walls
Where I can hold up my head and try to walk tall
No asking for money to buy personal things
A job for independence and all that it brings
A chance to meet people who don't talk baby talk
Go out for fun evenings or just for a walk
I'd like to contribute towards household bills
I have a need inside me, I have to fulfil
I love my family dearly, but I'm just not sure
If the life that I'm living is enough anymore
I want to be a wife, a mother, and a friend
But I also want to be, a person again.

Helen Bealing

VACANT STEPS

She walked along the road
Every day of the year
A little dog by her side.
She carried her shopping -
Enough for one,
And some food for her dog.
I often watched her progress,
Slow as it was,
Until she disappeared
Around the corner.
She held her head down
But she saw me
Once -
And smiled . . .
Until
One day
She didn't come down the road;
'Taken to hospital,'
The neighbourhood gossips proclaimed,
'Died in her sleep, poor love.'
And then they forgot
Her and her dog
And it seems only me
And the pavement
Miss their steps.

Clare Waterfield

MY GRANDDAUGHTER

I saw you first in a hospital cot
A small but priceless treasure
The beauty of your serene small face
Locked in my memory forever

I watched you quietly sleeping there
And I knew from the very start
You would be so special to me
And capture a place in my heart

With each new day I've seen you grow
Seen some tantrums and some tears
Watched you take those first few steps
With their knocks, bumps and fears

Your simple sounds and utterings
Very quickly changed to speech
You walk and talk with confidence
Now nothing's out of reach

As we explore your big new world
What a joy to hear you chat
The multitude of questions
But Granddad why? What for? What's that?

At present your character's forming
Your personality's playing its part
And when you give that special smile
You can melt a granddad's heart

The years pass by so quickly
But this I must confess
You always were and always will
Be my very own princess

If I could ask of anyone
To grant a wish I would
Be allowed a few more years to see
You blossom to womanhood.

R Davies

CONSUMED BY FEAR

Why do you only want to hurt?
Why don't you pity me?
A bitterness lives in your soul
for everyone to see.

I try to hide away from you
but sometimes you appear,
and even when you don't, my heart
is so consumed by fear.

There is no way that you will change
for you cannot be wrong,
and as you scream the things you do
you feel it makes you strong.

I've never spoken. It would be
like talking to a wall.
You wouldn't listen to a word
because you know it all.

You're satisfied and pleasured by
a soul that lives in pain,
for each time that I try to rise
you knock me down again.

There's fairness in hysteria
and justice in your cries,
and I must just accept your ways
bring weeping to my eyes.

The nightmare grows as years go by
and life's a constant fight.
I hope and pray with all my heart
an ending is in sight!

John Christopher

RED MOON

His eyes were red
His face was red
His hair was red,
A darkened tint of clotted blood,
the delta of a dried-up river on his head.
He looked into her eyes and said,

'Red Moon.'
She cocked her head.
'I'm looking for Red Moon.'

She touched his tattered shoulder
and her feelings bled.
He got up from his crouch. She led
him to a station bench.
She brought him tea,
And followed all the wanderings of a fuddled head,
the methylated spirit of a man who said,

'Red Moon.
I'm looking for Red Moon.'

He lay down on the bench.
She tucked her shopping bag beneath his head.
She left him there and went away
just long enough to find the man a bed.
An hour later she returned
and he was dead.

She took the crumpled photo from his hand.
She smoothed it out.
There was a young man's head.
She turned it over,
saw the words which read,

Red Moon.

Brian Iles

MR CARBUNCLE

Grumble, grumble, grumble, that's all we ever hear from Mr Carbuncle
'Why don't you keep your cat off my lawn and will you please shut
                          my back gate?' He yells to my uncle.
Uncle James, so quiet, must be a saint to remain cool and so very calm
Every time anybody approaches his car their presence set off an alarm.

Mr Carbuncle's adjectives are used exclusively by him
He conjures them up at will - he is bright, not at all dim;
He checks his change twice over - gives the shopkeepers merry hell
If they short change him he swears that he'll have them closed down -
                          they'll never again sell.

Fussy, fussy, fussy is Mr Carbuncle if you enter his house by the
                          front door -
You'll have to take off your shoes or you'll soil his polished floor;
'I have no time to waste going over things I've done before!'
'That man needs to have his head examined,' says Mother,
                          'He's becoming such a bore.'

Mr Carbuncle gave me five pounds last Christmas and demanded
                          a refund,
He wanted compensation for all the bad things to him which I
                          had done -
I called him Scrooge and told him that he should not be so mean
And peeked into his oven looking at the largest goose I'd ever seen.

'Don't you ever, don't you ever, don't you ever call me unjust and
                          a pain -
Whatever I say I'm right, perfect in fact, I'm not at all insane!'
But I've noticed that the only people who ever visit him are the
postmen, dustbin men, meter readers and people who wish to do
                          many a good deed -
And wonder if it is not just a waste of a life - such a sad existence
                          to lead.

Margaret Andrews

I WISH . . .

I wish, once more, that we could share
the memories I find so hard to bear;
a touch, caress: what I would not give
to again those happy days re-live

Then from this anguish and despair
I'd be free, uplifted, walking on air
to feel you near, close by my side,
sheer joy would in my heart abide
I wish . . .

The truth for feelings has no care
as in the face of reality I stare
and acknowledge what I know I must:
You are gone forever, just ashes and dust
is all that remains of our love affair
yet, I wish . . .

Claire Rolfe

A DAUGHTER

She came with the dawn
A bundle of joy, so lovely to behold
On a May day she was born
Into this great big world.

A treasure she is beyond compare,
Mischief is her middle name
Dancing eyes and fair hair
Very precious all the same.

She gladdens our hearts, this daughter of ours,
Where would we be without her
Giving all that life can give
Spreading happiness as she goes.

A ray of sunshine enters the room,
Bubbling over with laughter
Smiles and love dispel the gloom
For now and ever after.

Rita Douglas

THE PRETENDER

Her hair's been dyed so many times,
It looks like cotton wool,
She believes herself so wise,
But others see the fool.

A life of boredom she left behind,
She wants to have a good time,
Yet still she has no peace of mind,
Because she turned her hand to crime.

She yearns for a young man,
To keep her warm at night,
Everyone she captures,
Runs away with fright.

We all know she is middle-aged,
This she does deny,
If you say different she's in a rage,
With the norm' she doesn't comply.

She took up line-dancing,
And flung her feet up in the air,
It was the young man she was fancying
That really took her there.

She lives a life beyond her means,
And begs for others to look and see,
She can't afford the things she needs,
And wishes she could have them for free.

She has a house with many rooms,
A place she calls her home,
No matter how you try to reach her,
She still has no one to call her own.

Pauline Uprichard

ODE TO GEOFFREY

As part of my work I met an elderly man,
        who was distinguished, genteel and kind;
He had travelled a lot as a correspondent,
        a more worldly person you'd never find.

He contacted me to transcribe some tapes
        which he'd been dictating of his life's works,
For Reuters he was a correspondent during the war
        and his travelling was one of his perks.

Although the war was a series time
        he would only tell of its glories,
and wrote in such a wonderful way
        that it was fun typing his stories.

My geography had faded at this time,
        so I got out my atlas for knowledge,
And the notes we sent back and forth
        reminded me of time in college.

He seemed to enjoy educating me
        and was thrilled that I was interested,
But before we had time to meet in person
        He was hospitalised when his heart arrested.

I visited him at his bedside
        and he talked of his book being printed,
At 86 his body wanted to retire
        but his mind and soul never stinted.

So I'm helping colleagues who worked with him
        put his written articles together
So the world can remember this wonderful man
        and his memories will go on forever.

Judith Pryor

I MEDITATE

When I close my eyes and meditate
       It's wonderful what I see
I see my *Saviour Jesus Christ*
       By the waters of Galilee
I feel the light that shines so bright
       Caress my heart and soul
As the sun glints lightly on the waves
       My body *His* arms enfold
I look at *His* reflection
       In the waters near the edge
I see *God's* glory in *His* face
       The halo round *His* head
The harmony of angels singing
       Like a breeze caress the sea
Blends gently with the love I feel
       He gives so free to me
He is walking up the mountain path
       Crowds watching from below
They long to hear *Him speak the words*
       It's God's word they want to know
They pray that they may all be blessed
       That they may follow *Him*
To lead them from death's darkness
       To *His Kingdom* free from sin.

A S Price

WINDOW-DRESSING

Daintily she pats her piled-up hair
Of a dyed bright blondish hue.
For taste and fashion she has no flair
Though she's fairly well-to-do.

For her, some clichés spring to mind
Such as 'mutton dressed as lamb',
The figure? that is not streamlined.
In many ways she is a sham.

Uneducated, she tries to hide the fact,
Mis-quoting 'what the papers say'.
She has no finesse, she has no tact
And her jokes are oft risqué

Her make-up one would not call discreet
Regarding lipstick, blusher, powder.
Too brilliant for her small town street,
Combined with clothes - could not be louder.

She speaks in a simpering girlish voice
When trying to capture a man.
To listen, he often has no choice
Though to him she's an 'also ran'.

Can one call her an 'unclaimed blessing',
For as yet she's failed to find a mate
In spite of all her window-dressing
Time's running out, so it's p'raps too late.

Laura Föst

TIDAL

The tides are changing
The moon is waning
My hope is draining
The tides are changing
The moon is waxing
My star is rising, all my fear is subsiding
The bird soars in space, the stone is hurtled down to earth
Now I race ahead for the prize
Now a demon chases me, my terror reflected in his blazing eyes
And so the wheel of life turns me from stone to bird, from bird to stone
Today the winner, tomorrow the loser
Why must I waver from never losing sight of the end of the tunnel to
surrendering to the night?
Is an angel guarding me from danger or is a monster lurking behind
every corner?
Where is my faith?
Now I go forth into battle full of a sense of love and duty
Now I turn my back on the world and close my heart to mankind
Where is my anchor?
The tides are changing
I surrender meekly to their force as they surrender to the moon's,
their master.

Monica Gurney

PORTRAITS

Harry and Wills, two boys, no young men
In the public's eye again and again
As tots with their mum much love they were shown
Sadly gone from them now that they are both grown
Being a mother of boys my heart feels so much
At how they must miss her presence her touch
A fine example to others the way they've turned out
In them Diana lives on, there is no doubt
I admire their strength and I know they will be
Like their mother much loved by you and by me
It must make Prince Charles feel so proud just to know
His two fine young sons are adored wherever they go
Whatever they do in the future I'm sure
The nation's behind them for evermore
So good luck and God bless in my thoughts you will be
Dear Harry and Wills you're forever with me.

Anita Barnes

Tom

I glance to see if he's sitting there,
Bent and weatherbeaten.
Sitting in his regular chair,
Nothing to rest his feet on!

Yes he's there, he calls me over,
A twinkle in his eyes.
Said he'd always been a rover,
And he'd told many lies!

Skin hard and weatherbeaten,
His breath smells of stale beer.
Out of waste bins he had eaten,
Sometimes shed a silent tear.

His clothes are old and smelly,
His shoes are full of holes.
Never owned his own tele,
Never carried out his role.

His flat cap has lost its neb,
He's dirty and unshaven.
Never had a job he said,
His clothes, shiny like a raven.

His hands had a slight tremor,
He was now almost bald.
He was in a financial dilemma,
And no future did he hold.

Once young and dashing, now old and bent,
No one wants to know his story.
No food or money, can't pay his rent,
But he'll have his day of glory.

Gail Susan Halstead

CHILDHOOD

Little Snotty-nose would sit.
In her boots that didn't fit.
Matted curls stuck to her cheek.
Through the sticky fringe she'd peek.
Alone and dirty she would sit
On the step in the dusty street.

Worn-down shoes and holey socks
Navy knicks, elastic rot.
Matted jumper, cobbled darn,
Stranger's sweat mark under arm.
Little Snotty-nose would go.
Off to school and she would know.
Some of the other kids would laugh
And ask her had she had a bath.
Her mother's bath was made of tin.
Hung in the yard it made a din
But hardly ever ventured in.

Little Snotty-nose was happy,
Looked after her brother,
changed his nappy.
Sitting in his pram so sweet
Sticky bottle, brown swollen teat.
Sour curds soaking under his chin.
Big kiss from sister, shiny pink grin.

Playing hop-scotch till it's dark.
Can't even see the white chalk mark.
In for tea great chunks of toast.
See which one can eat the most.
Little Snotty-nose head bent.
Sits and reads to her heart's content.

Barbara Maddison

I KNOW AN OLD WOMAN

Gallant she is
Like some old liner
Breasting the squalls
of her own sea-life

Her losses are the landmarks
Determining her course
Death of parents, sister, husband
These she can discuss
With a lop-sided smile

But then I touched upon a central nerve
I asked her why she only had one child
And that long-held cargo of the years
Revealed itself in tears

And so I learned
About her ancient dream
Held still - deep within the hold
Embraced beneath her heart
Stillborn.

Dilly Parker

INHERITANCE

He sat astride his gleaming horse,
Jet-black it was and sixteen hands,
'Satan' by name - a fiery beast
With ears pricked and fierce eye
Yet gentled by this calm man's voice.

Born of long-ennobled stock
He was a soldier tall and straight
In stature and in character;
His service to his country
Disciplined and great
And, like so many, all unsung.

Beloved by him the quiet earth,
The woods and fields of his estates,
The tenants on his farms
And, too, a deep concern and generosity
For needs of the community
Around his gates.

Dearest of all, his wife and children
Who, when he came home, would run to him;
'My bundle of rags!' he'd shout with joy
And take them all in his wide open arms.
This Gentleman, who now long gone,
Passed on his code to his young four-
Of honour, duty, discipline of self,
Patriotism and respect of law,
Love of people, creatures, home
And, woven through it all wisdom
And a priceless sense of humour
And of fun.
How blessed, and how alike in character,
His younger son!

Margaret Willoughby

FRIEND OF MY LIFE

Come to me now,
You who is youthful, inspirational,
And fill my head with sweet compliments,
Come sit by me - and may your eyes
Shine with happiness,
- as they always will.
Tell me how much you love me
As you fold your weary muscles closer.
And I wonder if my eyes will ever
Shine like yours.
You hold me as a mother holds her first new-born,
And I fear my world might blow away
- when you are not near me.
I always live in hope
That you will never bade me goodnight
(like others)
Because I will be here for you
As the sun is shining.

Shelley Young

NO SAMARITAN

At Warren Street Station
On the opposite platform,
The girl stood doubled over in anguish,
Long silky hair hiding her face.
Tall, slender, android,
Clothed in the uniform of youth -
Jeans and black leather jacket,
She sobbed, cried, shrieked her grief,
Despair incarnate.
Leaning her back against the wall,
She slid down until she was propped
Knees to chest like a foetus in the sanctuary
Of her mother's womb
At Warren Street Station.

At Warren Street Station,
On the opposite platform,
People walked around her,
Averting their eyes as if
She had no part in their reality,
Passing by without seeing or caring.
I wanted to cross over and comfort her
But could think of nothing to say
Or do that would relieve her pain.
My train came and I went home,
Relieved next day to find that
Nobody had committed suicide,
Crushed to death under a train
On the tube network
At Warren Street Station.

Dora Stables

THE LIKENESS

An ode to the waitress, who served our Xmas dinner,
She might have coped better, had she been a bit thinner,
Struggling and squeezing between every table,
Oblivious to all for a while.
Her black dress matched her hair. She'd black glasses as well,
She could have been *'Male'* it was so hard to tell.
So many lines on her face. Not a hair out of place.
But unable to manage a smile.

She probably finished her work shift at nine,
And made pretty sure she got off on time.
Marching and stomping around like a horse
Champing her dentures between every course.

The likes of Dick Emery, you've never seen,
Could have been him returned to the scene,
His costume and make-up could not have done more
To match up to our waitress, that's for sure.

Although every action she did was on cue,
No-one could say, 'But I do *like* you!'
Before we could eat every last morsel,
We expected to hear, 'Eeh you are awful.'

It could well have been
His ghost from the past
Come to serve Xmas dinner
Right to the last.

Pat Hall

LISTEN TO ME

Love me, but don't spoil me
Tell me, but don't yell at me
Hold me, but don't keep me tied to you
Mind me, but don't wrap me in cotton wool
Show me how, but don't made a show of me
Correct me, but don't give in as soon as I cry
Listen to me, but don't make fun of my fears
Let me get dirty, but don't let me get nasty
Let me explore, but don't let me get lost
Let me kiss you, but don't make me kiss anyone
Encourage me, but don't bribe me
Forgive me, but don't forget to apologise
I'm like you, but don't try to make me the same.

E M Hughes

UNEXPECTED MEETING

It looks at me
With bulbous eyes,
Quite still at first
Small, wet, surprised,
Afraid to croak.

Initially, I'm scared,
But then I too
Am still, and we regard each other
With interest.

I see a dark body
Pulsating, head intent,
Neat, folded legs
Streamlined; and the whole
Well camouflaged.

And then I move.
His coiled spring uncoils,
He leaps to safety,
Brushing his cold, rough skin
Against my hand.

I scream; quite difficult
To believe that he
Is just a frog.

Ann Hiam

THE WIDOW GOLDEN-FIST

Her husband died and left her loded,
Fifteen years ago, they say;
Now tunes she plays on twinkling trinkets,
To keep her widow's woes at bay.

She rattles rings on every finger,
Jangles bangles round her wrist -
Such shimmer, shine and glitter, glitter,
From woeful Widow Golden-Fist.

Silver's fine but shines too coldly
And tarnishes too soon she fears:
Gleaming, golden comfort, only,
Dries a doleful widow's tears.

So shake her hand, or - take a bold line -
Kiss it and you'll find you've kissed
A hallmarked, eighteen-carat gold mine:
Weeping Widow Golden-Fist!

I White

JOAN JOHNSON

Joan is a joy to behold
Lacks nothing and is never bold
Enough to be thought unkind
A treasure to know in my mind.

Her neighbourly ways beguile
And freshens many, a friendly smile
Upon those who know her well
She is our dear friend a real swell!

Helpful when she is needed to fill in our day
At our Fellowship Club on a Tuesday
Sings like a nightingale
Songs of yesteryear with zeal.

May you Joan keep up the good work
Pretty as a picture, a cork
Of a lady, always giving
Kind answers to everyone's bidding.

Joan you are a good friend
To me, who feels the wind
Of friendship ever near
God be with you my friend dear.

Alma Montgomery Frank

HOLLIE'S FLOWERS

I love to see the flowers in her hair,
For it was I who put them there,
That cheeky smile and lovely dimple,
Oh why can't life be as simple,
For I wonder what the future holds
We have to watch while it unfolds,
'Hollie's Flowers' is my song
I love to walk in grasses long,
Just sit down while I take a snap,
A perfect day, with a map,
For unlike possessions she cannot be bought,
There's one small lesson she must be taught,
To love the plants and animals of our land,
Especially when so close to hand,
Let's hope the fields of joy stay green,
And learn to keep the country clean,
Hollie you are the apple of my eye,
I know my love will never die,
I would gladly give my life for you,
If you could turn those grey skies blue,
Your sweet innocence is a priceless gift,
You always give my days a lift.
Together let's make this world a better place,
So you can keep that smile upon your face.

Daren Peary

I WOULD IF I COULD

I'd be late for my own funeral
But only if I remembered.
I'd screw my head on tighter
If I hadn't been beheaded.
I'd be your greatest lover
If only I could turn you on.
I'd have had a lovely time
But only if I'd gone.
I'd watch the flowers bloom
But I forgot to plant the seeds.
I'll give you the kingdom
But I appear to have lost the deeds.
I'd buy you your dream car
But all my money's spent.
I'd lock you in my dream world
But the key's a bit bent.
I'd meet you from the train
But I can't find the station
I'd be deeply suicidal if I wasn't so elated.
I'd ring you at 4.40
But I can't find a phone box.
I'd climb Mount Everest
But I've lost my hiking socks.
I know I'm a little dizzy,
It's staring me in the face.
Will someone please look after
This terminally hopeless case?

Becky Uttley

MISSION ACCOMPLISHED

Blond hair, blue eyes, a saucy smile
        Michael is his name
Killing dragons, rescuing damsels
        Was his favourite game
'For England and St George'
        Would echo round the room
Who would have thought
        Our little knight would grow up quite so soon.

Six foot tall and handsome
        Is that our little boy
Not so very long ago he
        Was playing with a toy!

Kind and independent
        He has an inner strength
To achieve his aim in life
        He'll strive to any lengths.

Standing there so straight and tall
        With his companions, soldiers all
Marching, confidence in every stride
We felt that we could burst with pride.

To join the army was his dream
        Being part of an elite team
Well he's there, he's made the grade
        Today's his Passing Out Parade.

Rosemary Ann Betts

A PORTRAIT OF JESUS

Born in a cattle shed with no bed.
He was born of Mary so it's said.
Fled with his parents to Egypt's land.
Nothing there except miles of sand.
Became a carpenter like his dad.
Even when a child he was not bad.
Baptised by John then started his work.
His mission on earth he never shirked.
He said to man come follow me.
Then you can come and dwell with me.
Many followed but most did not.
When he moved on, most forgot.
What he had said about his dad.
He was happy and sometimes sad.
He healed the sick, the blind to see.
Still they crucified him on a tree.
He rose within three days of dying.
They said his disciples were just lying.
Many said he did not exist at all.
I said that, as I do recall.
Then I met with the Lord Jesus Christ.
And from that day he changed my life.
Above is a short portrait of the man.
Can I follow Jesus Christ? . . . Yes you can.

Don Goodwin

DADDY COME HOME

Will my daddy come today
Why did he have to go away,
Will he come I think he will
For I know he loves me still.

I wish he would come home to stay
Then in the garden we could play,
I can hardly wait until
I see him coming up the hill.

He said he'd come when he could
So I'll just wait and be good,
Does he know I miss him so
Did he really have to go.

I know he'll ring me on the phone
To tell me that he'll come back home,
Mommy said he's gone for good
Forget him - did you think I could.

S H G Johnson

SILENCE

No words from our mouths were spoken,
With sign language our words were said,
I know god above will welcome you,
As his words they can be read.

So we say good-bye dear Duncan,
In heaven above you will stay,
We will think about you quite often,
And meet again some day.

M R Smale

JACK OFALLTRADES

On Saturdays he's a pro' footballer
On Sundays a train driver.
On Mondays he's a policeman
On Tuesdays deep sea diver.
On Wednesdays he works in a chip shop
On Thursdays does meals on wheels.
And Friday's usually Jack's day off
Just depends on how he feels.

Stephen Dipré

GLENYS FREEMAN

If every friend could be just like you.
What a beautiful world this could be.
If every word was as sweet as yours.
What harm would it ever cause?
'Cos on the day you were born, an angel blessed this earth.
With a rare and special gift, and all that love is.
If only others knew what a friend like you could do.
Then maybe they'd understand how special it is to know you.

Amanda Jayne Biro

AUNTY LUCY

Can't stand my Aunty Lucy!
She's eccentric you know,
When she comes to visit
How the time passes slow.
'Here, have a peppermint,'
She says, quite haughtily,
And picks one from the bag
To stop me grabbing three!
That's what she told my mum,
But I would not do that,
So, who wants peppermints!
I'd rather eat my hat.

L M Wilson

WHAT A BEAUTIFUL TIME

We went for a walk one day,
Over the fields of hay.

We walked for a mile,
Then came to a stile.

We were walking and talking,
Humming and running, having a lovely time.

We came to a hill,
There we saw a windmill.

We climbed up the hill,
To investigate the mill.

What a wonderful view,
And we thought anew.

What a wonderful world this is,
God made it, and it is His.

Andrew S Taylor

SET

The sun bounced off his auburn curls and into his eyes,
The deep violet colour flared into life.
The colour that those eyes gave off,
Made his skin look golden and tanned.
His square chin gave his face a new-found accession,
But, the way that his lips curled around his words,
Made his face lose any love that had once hidden there.
His lips that form the words are as red as his blood,
But the words that he can say are evil.
An evil that can betray any trust,
Comes out of those violet eyes,
And once again the hatred leaves and the love comes back,
Just like an evil spirit had been injected into his soul.
His life has been taken over by a curse,
That will never leave his heart.

Jemma Howard

UNTITLED

Ding Dong there's the bell,
My meals on wheels are here,
Oh how nice it is to see Naomi,
We often share a tear.

Usually we laugh 'til we cry,
She really is a saint,
I don't always understand her,
Because her accent's quaint.

She comes from one of them 'ot places,
And finds England rather cold,
But when it comes to caring,
She knows how to carry the load.

If everyone was like her,
What a lovely place it would be,
With laughter and friendship abiding,
I'm alone and housebound you see.

Sheila J Hodgkins

THE DREAMER

He is a tall man, a slim man
Standing six feet four
Eyes of the bluest sky
Soft light brown hair
A smile warm enough to melt butter
Laughter bubbling, spilling from inside.
He walks with a smooth motion
Hands in pockets
With head tilted slightly down
As though he were worlds away,
Yet he misses nothing.
His soft spoken words
Cling to my heart
This is a kind man
A weak man
Tears flow easily from his eyes.
His dreams are hidden
Amongst everyday living
His heart holds secrets
That his mind shuts out
And his tongue won't speak.
He is trapped by his lies
Tortured and twisted,
Strange thoughts in his head.
His eyes burn with passion
Then flicker cold
As he hides his love
Beneath a shell of reality.

Tracey Goodman

RYAN GIGGS

Racy Goldenboy,
Riches Galore,
Rapidly Gallops,
Regally Glides.
Receives Gasps,
Reaps Glory,
Rouses Girls,
'Rather Gorgeous'.
Rugged Gem,
Radiates Games,
Reigns Godlike,
Ryan Giggs!

Jon Perigud

MR CLAUDE

He's camp, he's rough
He has that acquired unkempt look
He's successful, he's street-wise
The ladies they adore him
When he rolls those big brown eyes.

He tweaks and he teases
With his scissors he's a maestro
In his leathers with matching bag
He's de-rigeur, the latest fad
When he contemplates us in the mirror
We hold our breath and wait . . .
Yes he has the answer
Cut it here, cut it there
Those curls will have to go
What a marvel, what a miracle
The man we all love to know.

C M Berry

HAPPY, SAD AND THOUGHTFUL

You look so happy
Yet so sad
Though in a picture you should be glad
Or has the artist caught a part of you
That we don't see yet is very true.

You look so happy
Yet deep in thought
Which means he cannot paint while you are so distraught
Just talking a little might be fine
As he can paint while you think he is kind.

You look so happy
With the end
Was the sitting far too much time to spend
Or the finished work reminded you
Of an older painting hanging upon the landing too.

Keith L Powell

FATHER AND SON

I tried to copy what he did,
To copy what I saw.

When I was six, I remember
The way he left his spuds till last;

So did I.

The way he stood,
Hands thrust into pockets;

So did I.

The way he spoke,
Leaving h's off his words;

So did I.

He did 'odd-jobs' 'bout the house;
Using the strength of many.
Sawing, screwing, painting, burning,
If only I could too.

One summer, I remember
Using his heavy black blade and shaft,
He planted a willow,
To grow, he hoped,
To be as big and as strong as he.

That was then; this is now,
The hands that did so much,
Now all creased and puckered with age.

Like the willow outside;
Huddled and weathered with age.

He sits at the table,
I feed him;

Leaving his spuds till last.

John Summerville-Binks

STRIDING ACROSS THE LAND

You strode through our land
Stamping down on all who opposed.
You didn't hold out a helping hand
But walked along a lonely road.

You spent money as if it were water
For your own amusement and pleasure.
You made a martyr of your daughter,
Forgetting she'd once been your treasure.

You gathered scholars about you
But only the foreigners were safe.
Your close friends were very few,
Indigent people became starving waifs.

You strengthened the navy, building ships
Like the great Alfred did before,
But you never came to grips
With the realities behind your door.

There *were* people you could have trusted
But your suspicious nature didn't believe,
And the many women after which you lusted
Had reason enough to cry and grieve.

You could have been among the greats,
Well loved and praised in history,
But you chose to listen to unkind fates.
Why? That is an unsolved mystery!

Daf Richards

ROSES

Grandfather Thirkettle grew roses
Before he died
He even cut down the cherry tree
I loved as a child
A July evening when I saw
What he'd done
And on every side
Alba, Damask, Moss, Hybrid Tea
Each bush in flower
'I wanted to grow them all my life,'
He said on the lawn
Now I have
Now I have
The scent of roses and cigar.

Rosemary Muncie

STAND AND DELIVER

Black Bess stood under the old oak tree
On her back Dick waited patiently
Mask on face, his pistol held high
Stopped the coach as it came by.

Bold as brass yelled, 'Stand and deliver
Gentlemen please, your gold and silver.'
In the coach a Lord and Merchant
Escorting a Lady, her looks pleasant.

The Merchant handed over his purse
The Lord challenged with a curse,
'Before I'm robbed, blood will spill.'
Turpin fired, Black Bess stood still.

Blood ran down the wounded Lord's arm
'I'm sorry Madame, he said with charm
From your finger please the diamond ring.'
'Have it, for your deeds tonight you'll swing.'

'Goodnight.' Away the highwayman sped
A handsome reward put on his head.
Continued robbing with lots of luck
Fled to York where he became unstuck.

Harrold Herdman

WHAT MATTERS . . .?

If I was to think
What mattered to me
If I was to look and think and find
To smell and taste and feel and touch
To look through Oxford's advanced books
To search the seas and find a clue
Or to ask, what would matter to you?

I'd have to see, the landscapes around
The countries, cities and whatever else I found
To maybe compare
Or make a list
Take pictures so that I could not miss
A single thing, to take note of
Family bonds and friendly love
Children's laughter, shame and crime
Or other things in this life of mine

If I was to think
What mattered to me
I'd have to say it's what I see
The daily news and latest gossip
My family greetings and when friends all gather
To talk about anything, it never matters

The most important things to me
Are love, my friends and family.

Claire Wilson (15)

HYMN TO HIM

He.
Has golden grey hair.
With looks that I.
Would gladly die for.
He's taller than me.
With his pretty face.
A man to love.
To kiss and smile.
And make love to.
He's small in build.
Quite slim in fact.
I can see him now.
His picture is in my mind.
Like it always is now.
His blue eyes.
That seem to follow you around.
The lips.
To kiss away your blues.
The ears.
To nibble away at.
But most of all.
It's all of him.

J C Lewis

PORTRAIT OF A SPECIAL FRIEND

First impressions are not always right,
And yet I knew that somewhere deep within,
Though hurt, there lay a heart of gold,
That given time, your friendship I could win.

Brown hair, blue eyes, and weather-beaten face,
Upright and strong; someone whom trust inspires,
Steadfast; rock-like; an anchor in any storm,
So gentle, caring; you possess the nature I admire.

Your love for all things old, your patience
And persistence are talents not now often found,
Your affinity with small and helpless creatures
Shows the sincerity with which your life abounds.

The barriers you erected when first hurt
Are fading fast; the real man now I clearly see,
Each day brings forth yet another facet
Of the jewel you've turned out to be.

Beneath that rugged exterior, true beauty lies,
Compassionate, God-fearing, honest, too.
Finding joy in all the simple things in life -
I feel honoured having such a friend as you.

And should the time come when we have to part,
Called to our heavenly Master up above,
I shall give thanks for all that knowing you has meant,
Cushioned in this volatile world by your especial love.

Betty Robertson

To G M

To these islands two years ago
There came a man to us unknown,
His mission to make friend of foe
And minimise hatreds that have grown.

An American by choice and birth
Appointed then by his President
A man of integrity and worth
Who given a task will not relent.

To this benighted northern race
George Mitchell gave all his best
To bring extremists face to face,
But will *they* give peace its test?

B Wilson

THE CHILD WITHIN

If one could erase the memories
The reminders of long, long ago
Of a childhood so badly treated
Of a child with no love to show.
A child so young and innocent
With no-one to cuddle and hold
No love of the family around her
Pushed aside and left in the cold.
That child was sad and so lonely
As she grew older through the years
But the 'child' remained inside the woman
With the pain and so many tears.
The lonely years that followed
Still the pain and the scars to show
As she entered the doors of Sandville
A 'Haven' full of love n' hugs - you know.
It was a while before she accepted
That the people there really cared
For the 'child' within the woman
Was so alone and so very scared.
It was a long and a very hard 'battle'
As the 'child' blossomed and came through
With the help and love all around her
From her new family and friends it's true.
And so within this woman
That 'child' will always remain
With the memories buried within her
But knowing she'll never be alone again.

Sue Harper

LISALIKE

You are a library of unopened books.
Though your laughter rings volumes
And your tears splash tomes
It is the long between-these looks
When you are neither brightly teeter
Nor sigh-eye sad totemed-total -
It is when you are into yourself outerly
Creaming the iced-rose blushtint
Or pinking the calm of your closed anoint -
It is then, in the every utterly
You stem my restive ruffle of your leaves
With fragrant dust of chaptered mysteries.

Robin Lloyd

BEING BOLD

I gazed at her across the room,
Our eyes met, good and true.
I started and peered into the gloom,
And saw her hair was blue!

But on reflection it appeared
Not blue, but mauve and red,
Set up in spikes and really weird,
A rainbow on her head!

She wore a multi-coloured dress,
And struck an adult pose,
She really did look quite a mess,
With four rings in her nose!

The colours were for all to see,
In stripes of equal size,
I had to know - it still bugged me -
But was it really wise?

My fascination would not hold,
I took a gulp of beer,
And then I strode up very bold,
'Is that your own hair. Dear?'

June Beadnell

INFORMATION

We hope you have enjoyed reading this book - and that you will continue to enjoy it in the coming years.

If you like reading and writing poetry drop us a line, or give us a call, and we'll send you a free information pack.

Write to :-
Poetry Now Information
1-2 Wainman Road
Woodston
Peterborough
PE2 7BU
(01733) 230746